ANCIENT ANIMALS

Eryops (AIR-ee-ops)

by
Suzanne Francis

with
Matthew T. Carrano, Ph.D.
Consultant

Scholastic Inc.

New York Toronto London Auckland Sydney
Mexico City New Delhi Hong Kong Buenos Aires

ISBN 0-439-83876-2

Designers: Bob Budiansky and Lee Kaplan.

Cover illustration: *Smilodon* © Jaime Chirinos.

Title page: *Eryops* © Stephen Missal;
(swamp background) © Wendy Sue Gilman/Shutterstock.com.

Back cover illustration: *Megatherium* © Jaime Chirinos.

All Ty the *Tyrannosaurus rex* illustrations by Ed Shems.

All 3-D conversions by Pinsharp 3D Graphics.

Interior Photo and Illustration Credits:
Page 4: *Smilodon* © Jaime Chirinos.
Pages 6–7: (*Dimetrodon* skeleton) © Kris Kripchak; *Lystrosaurus* © Melissa Frankford;
    (*Diatryma* skeleton) © Kris Kripchak; *Basilosaurus* © H. Kyoht Luterman.
Page 8: *Thysanopeltis* © Todd Marshall.
Page 9: *Meganeuropsis* and *Arthropleura* © Karl Huber.
Page 10: All illustrations © Karl Huber.
Page 11: (*Eryops* skeleton) © Kris Kripchak.
Pages 12–13: *Helicoprion* © Karl Huber; (fossil shark tooth) © Ismael Montero Verdu;
    Ctenacanthus © Julius Csotonyi; coelacanth © H. Kyoht Luterman.
Page 14: *Dimetrodon* © Todd Marshall.
Page 15: *Proganochelys* © Jaime Chirinos.
Page 16: (*Iberomesornis* fossil) © Roy Lomas/PhotographersDirect.com; *Patagopteryx*
    © Jaime Chirinos; (cloud forest) © SF Photography/Shutterstock.com.
Page 17: *Tanystropheus* © Karl Huber.
Pages 18–19: *Deinosuchus* and *Simosuchus* © Stephen Missal.
Pages 20–21: All illustrations © H. Kyoht Luterman; (jungle) © Dhoxax/Shutterstock.com.
Page 22: All illustrations © Stephen Missal.
Page 23: *Ambulocetus* © H. Kyoht Luterman.
Pages 24–25: (Icy mountains) © Dmitry Lavruhin/Shutterstock.com; woolly mammoths
    © Stephen Missal.
Pages 26–27: (*Smilodon* skeleton) © Kris Kripchak; *Smilodon* illustration © Todd Marshall.
Page 28: *Megatherium* © Jaime Chirinos.
Page 29: All illustrations © Stephen Missal.
Page 30: (Christian Sidor) © Cecelia Mortenson, photo courtesy of Christian Sidor.
Page 31: *Panochthus* © Todd Marshall.
Page 32: (Ground sloth skeleton) © Kris Kripchak.

12 11 10 9 8 7 6 5 4 3 2   7 8 9 10 11/0

Printed in the U.S.A.

First Scholastic printing, August 2006

TABLE OF CONTENTS

WELCOME TO

Smilodon
(SMILE-loh-don)

ANCIENT ANIMALS!

Hi, it's your best dino bud, Ty! Are you ready for a new prehistoric adventure? Today we're going to meet some amazing animals, but they aren't dinos! Yup, dinos weren't the only animals alive during the Mesozoic. And there were tons of animals on Earth before and after us dinos came to town, too. Did you know that:

Ty
Tyrannosaurus rex
(tie-RAN-oh-SOR-uhss
RECKS)

◆ Some prehistoric birds were taller than most basketball players?

◆ There was a whale that could walk?

◆ There was a bug that was longer than a rattlesnake?

And we'll answer all kinds of interesting questions like:

◆ What were the first kinds of animals to live on Earth?

◆ Are there any ancient animals still around today?

◆ What kinds of animals were alive during the Ice Age?

Remember, when you see this icon, put on your **3-D glasses** to make the pictures jump right off the page!

Are you ready to meet some ancient animals? Follow the footprints and let's go!

Did you know that the Earth has been around for a really *long* time? Scientists think that the Earth is 4½ billion years old.

4½ billion? That's a lot!

Paleozoic
542–252 million years ago

Modern animals first showed up in the **Paleozoic Era** about 542 million years ago. Life in this era first started out in the seas, with critters like fish and shellfish, but plants and animals eventually made their way to dry land. Toward the end of the Paleozoic, four-legged animals like **Dimetrodon** (die-MEET-troh-don) appeared (see page 14), but there were no mammals (see page 20) or birds. At the very end of the Paleozoic, the largest extinction in Earth's history occurred. Scientists think that 90 percent of all animals in the sea died out.

Mesozoic
252–65 million years ago

The **Mesozoic Era** started 252 million years ago after the Paleozoic ended and is known as "The Age of Reptiles," since reptiles ruled the air, land, and sea. While animals like dinosaurs, pterosaurs, and marine reptiles got bigger and bigger in the middle of the Mesozoic, the first mammals and birds appeared. The Mesozoic ended 65 million years ago when another large extinction wiped out the dinos and other animals.

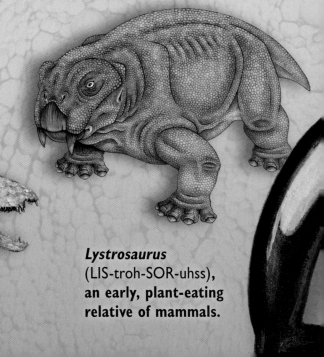

Lystrosaurus (LIS-troh-SOR-uhss), **an early, plant-eating relative of mammals.**

Dimetrodon **skeleton**

PREHISTORIC LIFE

While the Earth is 4½ billion years old, modern animals only appeared on Earth about 542 million years ago. Scientists divide up this time into three eras: the **Paleozoic** (PAIL-lee-oh-ZOE-ik), the **Mesozoic** (MEZZ-oh-ZOE-ik), and the **Cenozoic** (SEN-oh-ZOE-ik). Take a look at the chart below and find out more about these three eras and the amazing animals that lived during them.

Cenozoic
65 million years ago – present

The **Cenozoic Era** began 65 million years ago and still continues on today. The Cenozoic is sometimes called "The Age of Mammals" since that's what the largest animals are, but other kinds of life appeared as well. For one thing, birds really took off in the Cenozoic, with huge ones like **Diatryma** (DIE-uh-TRY-muh), as well as the birds that we see around today.

This era is famous for its ice ages (page 24), along with a few ancient animals like woolly mammoths and saber-toothed cats.

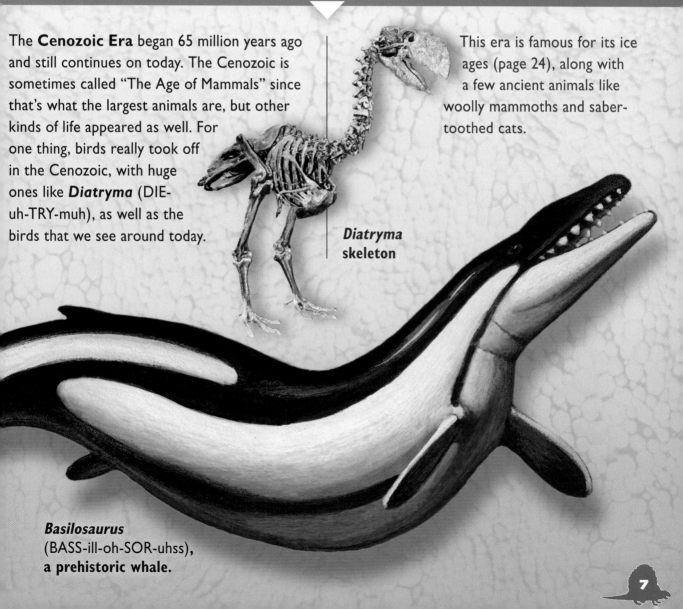

Diatryma skeleton

Basilosaurus (BASS-ill-oh-SOR-uhss), **a prehistoric whale.**

The **Paleozoic Era** began 542 million years ago and boy, did the Earth look different back then!

But wasn't it boring without any dinos?

No way! The Paleozoic was exciting because all kinds of life were just starting out. For the first time ever, the Earth was home to fish, plants, bugs, reptiles, and more! Read on to discover some of the first critters that ever walked the Earth.

Wacky Invertebrates

The Paleozoic is sometimes called "The Age of **Invertebrates**" (in-VUR-tuh-brits) because these wacky creatures really rocked this era. Check out these pages for more info on the weird world of invertebrates.

TRILOBITES

Trilobites (TRY-loh-bites) were around since the start of the Paleozoic. They were marine invertebrates and lived just about everywhere in the ocean. Scientists have found more than 15,000 kinds! Most trilobites were only 2–3 inches (5–8 cm) long, but some could grow up to 2 feet (½ m) long!

Trilobites' mouths were underneath their bodies, so they ate in a wacky way. They had lots of legs that stirred up tasty morsels as they moved across the ocean floor. Then their mouths would suck the tidbits right up like a prehistoric vacuum cleaner!

Thysanopeltis (thigh-SAN-oh-PELT-tiss), **a trilobite**

Dino Dictionary

An *invertebrate* is an animal without a backbone.

Bug Off!

Usually a bug is no big deal, but in the Paleozoic, that wasn't always true. Some prehistoric insects were huge! Check out the bugs below and see for yourself.

MEGANEUROPSIS

Meganeuropsis (MEG-ah-ner-OP-sis) had the biggest wings of any insect ever. This giant dragonfly had a wingspan that reached 2½ feet (1 m). *Meganeuropsis* was five times the size of the biggest dragonfly alive today!

ARTHROPLEURA

At 6 feet (2 m) long, *Arthropleura* (AR-throh-PLUR-uh) was one big bug! This gigantic, millipede-like insect had up to 30 pairs of legs and a tough body covering that helped protect it from predators. *Arthropleura* lived in swampy forests and was an **herbivore** (ER-bih-VORE). This big bug feasted on meals of rotting leaves and plants. Yummy!

Meganeuropsis

Arthropleura

> **Dino Dictionary**
> An *herbivore* is an animal that only eats plants.

Oddballs

Sometimes scientists find a really cool prehistoric invertebrate, but they have no idea what group of animals it belongs to! Sneak a peek at some Paleozoic oddballs that lived 530–540 million years ago—some of the first critters to crawl the Earth!

WIWAXIA

Wiwaxia (wih-WAX-zee-uh) was a weird invertebrate that grew up to 2 inches (5 cm) long. *Wiwaxia* had two rows of spines down its back, which probably kept predators away. Scientists aren't quite sure what *Wiwaxia* was, but they think it might be related to earthworms, or to shellfish and snails.

HALLUCIGENIA

Hallucigenia (huh-LOOSE-sih-JEN-ee-uh) had a set of clawed tentacles on one side of its body and two sets of long, moving spines on the other. At first, some scientists thought that this creature walked on its spines, while others figured *Hallucigenia* was a piece of a bigger animal. By 1991, scientists agreed that *Hallucigenia* walked on its tentacles and used its spines for protection. But there's still one thing they don't know: where's *Hallucigenia*'s head?

OPABINIA

Opabinia (OH-pah-BIN-nee-ah) was about 3 inches (8 cm) long, and had five mushroom-shaped eyes and excellent eyesight. It had spines and a long, flexible **proboscis** (proh-BOSS-kis) with a pincer that was probably used for grabbing prey. *Opabinia* could've stuck its nifty proboscis into the sand to hunt for worms and then snatched them up with its pincer.

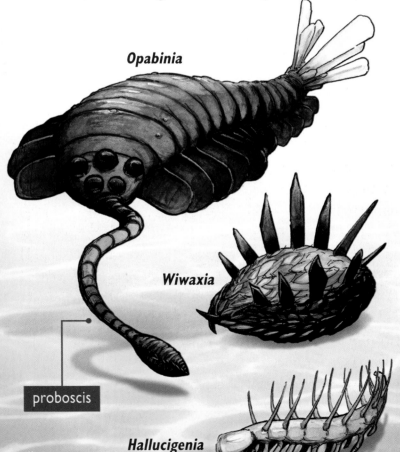

Opabinia

Wiwaxia

proboscis

Hallucigenia

Dino Dictionary

A *proboscis* is a long, flexible nose that animals usually use to eat with, like an elephant's trunk.

Eryops skeleton

Amazing Amphibians

Some creatures that swam in Paleozoic waters also spent time on land: **amphibians** (am-FIB-ee-uhns). Check out this huge amphibian!

ERYOPS

Eryops (AIR-ee-ops) was a 5-foot (1½-m) long amphibian that lived in swamps 250 million years ago. *Eryops* had a flat, triangle-shaped skull that grew as long as 2 feet (½ m)! It had a huge mouth with lots of teeth and strong jaws. Its thick body, short tail, and short legs definitely weren't built for speed. Some scientists think *Eryops* couldn't run at all!

Even though it was a slowpoke, *Eryops* was a fierce predator. It hunted and ate fish, small reptiles, and other amphibians. *Eryops* ate like a croc does today—it grabbed its prey in its mouth and threw its head back to gulp it down.

Dino Dictionary

An *amphibian* is a cold-blooded animal with a backbone. It lives in water during its early life and on land as an adult. Newts, frogs, and salamanders are amphibians.

The Skinny on Sharks

Sharks have been prowling the oceans for a long time—more than 350 million years! Lots of different kinds of sharks swam in the Paleozoic ocean. Read on and learn about two ancient hunters of the deep.

Helicoprion

HELICOPRION

Helicoprion (HEEL-ih-koh-PRY-on) was a 10-foot (3-m) long predator whose teeth had a twist! This shark had a toothy spiral on its lower jaw with special flat teeth that crushed shellfish and other invertebrates. *Helicoprion*'s teeth didn't fall out like other sharks' teeth do. Instead, new teeth grew in from the back of the mouth and pushed all the older teeth to the center of the coil.

DINO DATA

Prehistoric and modern-day sharks have replaceable teeth, just like dinos did. But a shark's jaws are way different than a dino's! Instead of one row of teeth, sharks have lots of rows of teeth. When a shark loses a tooth from the front row, a tooth from the row behind moves forward to replace it. That way, a shark always has a full set of choppers.

Fossil shark tooth

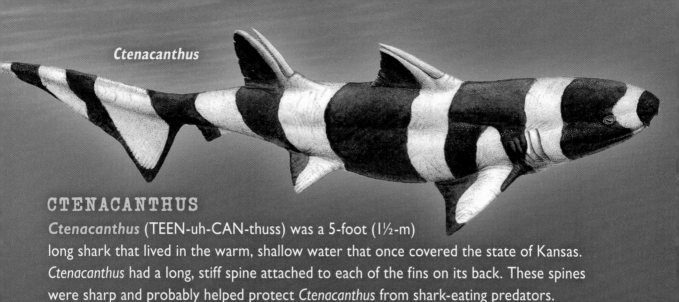

Ctenacanthus

CTENACANTHUS

Ctenacanthus (TEEN-uh-CAN-thuss) was a 5-foot (1½-m)
long shark that lived in the warm, shallow water that once covered the state of Kansas.
Ctenacanthus had a long, stiff spine attached to each of the fins on its back. These spines
were sharp and probably helped protect *Ctenacanthus* from shark-eating predators.

Catch of the Day

Other fish showed up during the Paleozoic,
too. Check out one of the first fish to
come to the Paleozoic party!

Coelacanth

COELACANTH

In 1938, a fisherman in the Indian
Ocean caught a weird-looking fish. Just
before he sold it, a scientist named Marjorie
Courtenay-Latimer looked at it and couldn't
believe her eyes! The fish was a **coelacanth** (SEEL-
luh-kanth)—which was supposed to have gone extinct
millions of years ago! Since then, more coelacanths have
been found. They live where few other fish do—400–
700 feet (122–213 m) below the surface of the ocean.
To catch prey, coelacanths open their mouths and suck
in water, fish, and any other tasty treats in their path. They have a special joint that allows

Funny Bones

Q: Why couldn't the coelacanth
keep a secret?

A: Because it had a big
mouth!

Dimetrodon

Smooth Sailing

Along with invertebrates, amphibians, and sharks, reptiles also appeared in the Paleozoic. Check out the unusual reptile on this page!

DIMETRODON

Dimetrodon (die-MEET-troh-don) was a reptile that lived 280 million years ago. It weighed about 500 pounds (227 kg), and was longer than a car! Its teeth were strong and sharp which made them great for stabbing and slicing meat. Yup, you guessed it, *Dimetrodon* was a **carnivore** (KAR-nih-VORE).

See that big flap of skin with long, bony spines on *Dimetrodon*'s back? Some scientists think that this flap, or "sail," helped *Dimetrodon* stay warm or keep cool. This reptile could park it in the sun or shade to heat up or chill out. The sail also could have scared away predators by making *Dimetrodon* look bigger than it was, or helped it to find a mate.

Dino Dictionary

A *carnivore* is an animal that only eats meat.

MOSEY THROUGH THE MESOZOIC

Next in our prehistoric travels is the **Mesozoic Era**, which began 252 million years ago. You might know that dinosaurs ruled back then, making this era "The Age of Reptiles."

But dinos weren't the only animals making a splash. Birds, reptiles, and mammals were shaking things up, too. Let's take a look at some of the amazing animals that lived next door to dinos!

Seems like it was just yesterday!

Shelling Out

Turtles first appeared in the Mesozoic, but some of them were a bit different than the ones you'd see hanging out in a pond today. Check out the very spe-*shell* animal below!

PROGANOCHELYS

Proganochelys (pro-GAN-noh-KEEL-ees) is the first known turtle. It was like today's turtles since it was toothless and had a protective shell on its back. But unlike its modern-day relatives, this turtle had sharp spikes covering its neck and its long, spiky tail ended in a bony club. *Proganochelys* couldn't hide inside its shell like turtles do today. It needed all that armor to protect itself. This prehistoric turtle lived near ponds and other small bodies of water, but it probably spent most of its time on land.

Funny Bones

Q: How do turtles call each other?

A: With their *shell* phones!

Proganochelys

Early Birds

The first birds showed up 150 million years ago during the Mesozoic and shared the Earth with dinos. Check out the two early birds below.

IBEROMESORNIS

Iberomesornis (eye-BER-oh-mes-OR-nis) was about the size of a sparrow with a wingspan of about 8 inches (20 cm). Like its modern-day cousins, *Iberomesornis* had feathery wings that weren't just for show. This bird could fly! But unlike today's birds, *Iberomesornis* had a curved claw on each wing. *Iberomesornis* was probably an **omnivore** (AHM-nih-vore), and would eat just about anything it could stuff in its beak!

An *Iberomesornis* fossil at life-size. The coin is about as big as a U.S. nickel.

Dino Dictionary

An *omnivore* is an animal that eats both plants and animals.

PATAGOPTERYX

Patagopteryx (PAT-uh-GOP-teh-ricks) was a Cretaceous bird about the size of a modern-day chicken. But you'd never find *Patagopteryx* perched in a tree! It had small wings and wasn't able to fly. So how did this prehistoric bird get around? *Patagopteryx* had long legs, so it could run fast to escape predators and catch meals of fish and insects.

Patagopteryx

Beach Bum

Not all big reptiles were dinos back in the Mesozoic. Check out the long-necked reptile below!

TANYSTROPHEUS

Tanystropheus (TAN-ee-STROH-fee-uhss) was a reptile that lived during the Late Triassic, 235 million years ago. And look at that neck! One kind of *Tanystropheus* had a neck that was 10 feet (3 m) long—longer than a modern-day giraffe's neck. But with only 10 neck **vertebrae** (VUR-tuh-bray), *Tanystropheus*'s neck wasn't very flexible.

> ### Dino Dictionary
> **Vertebrae** are the small bones that make up the neck and backbone.

Tanystropheus was a carnivore and feasted on insects, small reptiles, fish, and squid. This reptile might've spent some time in the water, but it probably hung out on the beach a lot and used its long neck to go fishing!

What do you think they used as bait?

Tanystropheus

Crocs Rock

Another group of animals that were new to the Mesozoic enjoyed life on land and water like *Proganochelys* (page 15): crocodiles! But these crocs weren't much like the ones hanging around today. Read on and you'll see why!

DEINOSUCHUS

Deinosuchus (DIE-noh-SUE-kuss) lived in North America and was one of the largest crocodiles ever. Its name means "terrible crocodile" and it's easy to see why. This croc was 30–40 feet (9–12 m) long and could weigh up to 5 tons. *Deinosuchus* was as long as a *T. rex*!

Deinosuchus was a carnivore and probably ate large fish, reptiles, and even dinosaurs. This giant croc might have waited in the water for an animal to come and take a drink. Then it grabbed its prey with its huge jaws and dragged it into the water and dinner was served!

That's T-riffic!

SIMOSUCHUS

Simosuchus (SEE-moh-SUE-kuss) was about 5 feet (1½ m) long and weighed around 250 pounds (113 kg). With its short, stubby snout and round head, *Simosuchus* was definitely not your average croc. Instead of a mouth full of sharp, pointy teeth, *Simosuchus* had small teeth that looked like they belonged to an iguana. Why? *Simosuchus* was an herbivore, which makes it one of the few plant-eating crocodiles ever discovered! This small croc probably lived mostly on land in Madagascar and couldn't swim long distances. *Simosuchus* had thick plates on its back and stomach to help protect it from predators. It might have been able to hide by burrowing in dirt or mud, too.

DINO DATA

Crocodiles are cold-blooded like snakes, lizards, and turtles. This doesn't mean that their blood is actually cold. It means that their body temperature depends on their surroundings. This is why today's crocs like to live in warm places.

Simosuchus

Deinosuchus

Marvelous Mammals

Some other incredible animals showed up for the first time and lived with dinos: **mammals** (MAM-uhls). Meet the two marvelous mammals below!

FRUITAFOSSOR

Fruitafossor (FROOT-uh-FOSS-or) was discovered in 1998 when a nearly complete fossil was found in Fruita, Colorado. This 6-inch (15 cm) long mammal was tiny—it wasn't even as long as a pencil! It lived during the Late Jurassic, 150 million years ago.

Dino Dictionary

Mammals are animals that are mostly covered in hair, give birth to live babies, and make milk for them. People, dogs, and bears are all mammals.

DINO DATA

Small animals are harder to find because their bones don't fossilize as well as larger animals. Most of the time, scientists only find their teeth or jaws.

Scientists noticed that *Fruitafossor* had super-strong arms for its size. They nicknamed this little critter "Popeye," after a famous cartoon about a spinach-eating sailor. *Fruitafossor* probably used its strong forearms and claws to dig for termites' nests and other invertebrates. It's the oldest known mammal to eat this way.

Fruitafossor

Do you think *Fruitafossor* liked bug-sicles?

Sinodelphys

SINODELPHYS

In 2003, an exciting fossil was found in China. It was a nearly complete skeleton of a *Sinodelphys* (SYE-noh-DEL-fiss) that was about 125 million years old! Scientists were psyched about *Sinodelphys* because it's the oldest known relative of **marsupials** (mar-SOO-pee-uhls).

Dino Dictionary

Marsupials are mammals that have pouches where their babies stay for protection. Kangaroos, opossums, and koalas are some marsupials that are alive today.

Sinodelphys was about 6 inches (15 cm) long and only weighed about an ounce (28 g). That's less than five U.S. quarters! This tiny mammal dined on insects and worms.

Q: What do you call a lazy marsupial?
A: A *pouch* potato!

Sinodelphys's feet and legs were great for climbing. It could climb the lower branches of trees and bushes and probably spent most of its time hanging out there, hiding from hungry meat-eating dinosaurs!

THE SENSATIONAL CENOZOIC

The **Cenozoic Era** started 65 million years ago after the Mesozoic ended. During the Cenozoic, the weather changed from hot and muggy all the time to nice and cool, and the Earth started having seasons. With these changes and the extinction of dinos and many other animals, a whole new world of plants and animals appeared.

This bird could really stomp around!

Diatryma

DIATRYMA

Diatryma (DIE-uh-TRY-muh) was a powerful, meat-eating bird about 7 feet (2 m) tall. Its huge head had a big, hooked beak over a foot (30 cm) long! *Diatryma*'s wings were way too small to lift its giant body into the air. Instead, this bird had strong, dinosaur-like legs that were made for strolling.

Phorusrhacus

PHORUSRHACUS

Phorusrhacus (FOR-uhss-RAKE-uhss) was another huge, flightless bird that was 5 feet (1½ m) tall. Like *Diatryma*, this bird had a very large head with a sharp, eagle-like beak and wasn't a flier. *Phorusrhacus* was a carnivore and probably ate anything it could chase down, including reptiles, mammals, and other birds.

DINO DATA

Phorusrhacus was part of a group of birds known as the "terror birds." Even though they couldn't fly, these meat-eating birds were scary! They chased down prey and snapped it up in their claws or beaks. Scientists think that this terror bird could have swallowed prey as big as a beagle in one gulp.

A Whale of a Good Time

Since prehistoric times, whales have changed more than any other mammal. Check out this incredible Cenozoic whale!

AMBULOCETUS

Believe it or not, this furry, four-legged creature is thought to be one of the earliest whales. By looking at its teeth, nose, and ears, scientists know that *Ambulocetus* (AM-byu-loh-SEE-tuhss) was an ancestor of today's largest animals. The name *Ambulocetus* means "walking whale." Yup, scientists think that *Ambulocetus* could use its arms and legs to walk on land.

But *Ambulocetus* could probably swim much faster than it could walk. This prehistoric mammal was only about the size of a sea lion. It had long, strong jaws and shark-like teeth and it probably could hear underwater, just like modern-day whales do.

Ambulocetus

Q: Why did the *Ambulocetus* say "thank you"?

A: Because it was *whale-mannered!*

Chill Out! Life in the Ice Age

About 2½ million years ago, the weather on Earth began to get chilly. It got so cold that sheets of ice called **glaciers** (GLAY-shurs) began to form. By the beginning of the **Pleistocene Epoch** (PLICE-toe-seen EHP-puck), almost one-third of the whole Earth was covered in snow and sheets of ice. That's why some people call the Pleistocene the "**Ice Age**."

During the Ice Age, animals like saber-toothed cats and woolly mammoths walked the Earth. Check out the next few pages to find out what life was like in the deep freeze.

Dino Dictionary

An *ice age* is a period of time when glaciers grow larger and cover more of the Earth. Although most people think there was only one ice age, there were lots of ice ages in prehistoric times with periods of warm weather in between. The last ice age started 100,000 years ago and lasted for 90,000 years.

Who turned off the heat?

WOOLLY MAMMOTH

A **woolly mammoth** (WOOL-lee MAM-muth) was a huge mammal that was related to modern-day elephants. It grew up to 11 feet (3 m) tall and weighed up to 3 tons. That's as heavy as 130 human adults! Woolly mammoths were all set for icy weather. They had very thick skin, and their fur was made up of hairs 3 feet (1 m) long.

WHAT CAUSES AN ICE AGE?

A bunch of different things happen when an ice age starts. First, the weather gets colder and it snows a lot, and all that snow turns to ice. Once there's enough ice, the ice reflects sunlight and keeps the Earth from heating up, making it even colder. The colder it gets, the more ice that forms, so soon most of the Earth is covered in ice. Sometimes changes in ocean currents, or the location of the continents can help start or end an ice age, too.

Unlike elephants, which have big ears to help them cool off, woolly mammoths had small ears. Small ears let less heat out, and they helped keep woolly mammoths warm. Even though they had huge tusks up to 13½ feet (4 m) long, all mammoths were herbivores. Scientists think these animals spent up to 20 hours a day eating grass, leaves, and branches. Their giant tusks were probably used for protection and helped them root around in the snow for food.

BABY EFFIE

Scientists have learned more about the woolly mammoth than any other extinct prehistoric mammal because they've discovered lots of fossils that are more than just bones. Since mammoths often died in icy places, their bodies froze and were preserved for thousands of years. In 1948, a fossil woolly mammoth was found near a gold mine in Alaska. The fossil mammoth was less than a year old when it died and was nicknamed "Effie." Effie was so well-preserved that scientists were able to study her skin and muscles.

SMILODON

Smilodon (SMILE-loh-don) was a big prehistoric cat that was 5 feet (1½ m) long, 3 feet (1 m) tall, and weighed as much as 800 pounds (363 kg). Its two 7-inch (18-cm) long side teeth, or **saber** (SAY-bur) teeth, were as long as a *T. rex*'s!

Smilodon's teeth were as big as mine?

Dino Dictionary

A *saber* is a heavy sword with a curved blade. Can you guess why scientists call *Smilodon* a "saber-toothed" cat?

With its big body and short legs and tail, *Smilodon* couldn't run fast like a cheetah or lion. But it was a serious predator that could pounce on its prey when they weren't looking. *Smilodon* probably hid and waited for an animal to come close, and then attacked. It could open its jaws almost twice as wide as today's lions. Most scientists think that *Smilodon* lived in packs the way today's lions do, too.

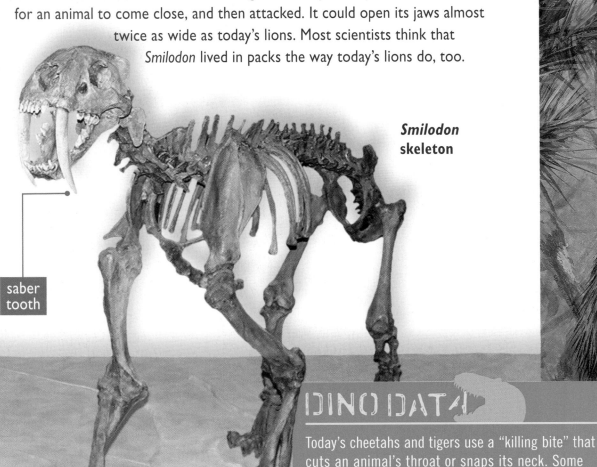

Smilodon skeleton

saber tooth

DINO DATA

Today's cheetahs and tigers use a "killing bite" that cuts an animal's throat or snaps its neck. Some scientists think that *Smilodon* used its teeth to grab and hold on to prey, like these cats do. Other scientists think that saber teeth were used to give a deadly wound to the prey's belly or throat. *Smilodon* might have given its prey one big stab, let go, and then waited for it to die.

LIFE'S THE PITS

Have you heard of the **La Brea Tar Pits**? The La Brea Tar Pits are a huge fossil site for Ice Age animals in Los Angeles, California. A tar pit forms when crude oil oozes up from underground and makes a puddle. After a while, the crude oil gets thick and sticky and becomes tar or **asphalt** (AS-fawlt). If an unlucky animal stepped in a few inches of this super-sticky goo, it was really stuck! Since it couldn't escape, the animal died and its bones sunk into the tar, which preserved them for millions of years. The La Brea Tar Pits were a sticky end for many ancient animals. Lots of well-preserved fossils have been found there, including woolly mammoths and *Smilodon*.

Smilodon

Slow Motion Sloths

Some animals back in the Cenozoic liked to take things slow. Take a peek at this super-sized animal that was a real Cenozoic slowpoke.

MEGATHERIUM

Megatherium (MEG-uh-THEER-ee-um) was a huge ground sloth that lived 2 million years ago. At 20 feet (6 m) long and weighing 3–4 tons, Megatherium was as big as an elephant—and 10 times bigger than any sloth alive today. Because of the big, curved claws on its fingers and toes, Megatherium walked on the sides of its hands and feet. Scientists think that Megatherium used its hand claws to hook branches and bring fruit or leaves toward its mouth. Then it pulled the goodies off with its long tongue.

DINO DATA

Today's sloths look and act very differently than their Cenozoic cousins, like Megatherium. For one thing, modern-day sloths spend most of their time hanging out in trees, resting. Some of today's tree sloths move so slowly that they even grow moss in their fur!

A group of
Megatherium

Ancient Aussies

By the beginning of the Cenozoic Era, Australia had become the big island that it still is today. Lots of strange animals appeared in Australia that lived nowhere else on Earth. Check out these two awesome Aussies!

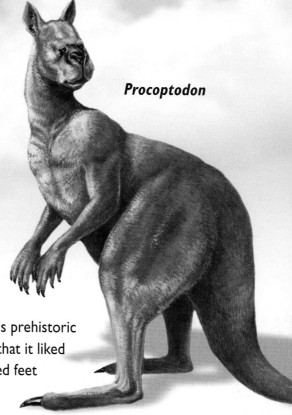

Procoptodon

PROCOPTODON

Procoptodon (proh-COP-toe-don) was a short-faced kangaroo that lived 1½ million years ago. *Procoptodon* could grow to more than 8 feet (2 m) tall, making it the largest known kangaroo.

But unlike its kanga-cousins, *Procoptodon* had long claws on the end of two fingers. Scientists think that this prehistoric kangaroo used these claws to pull down high branches that it liked to munch on. *Procoptodon* also hopped along on one-toed feet that were like hooves.

Thylacoleo

THYLACOLEO

Even though *Thylacoleo* (THIGH-lah-coh-LEE-oh) looked a lot like a modern-day tiger, it was a marsupial (see page 21). Some kinds of *Thylacoleo* were as small as a house cat, but others were as big as a lion and weighed up to 360 pounds (163 kg).

Thylacoleo was a carnivore and a fierce predator. It could grab and slash prey with its long claws, and it had super-strong jaws and sharp teeth for slicing through meat.

Funny Bones

Q: How did *Procoptodon* sneeze?
A: Kanga-choo!

Q + A

PALEONTOLOGIST
CHRISTIAN SIDOR

Meet Christian Sidor, a paleontologist with the Burke Museum of Natural History and Culture in Seattle, Washington. Dr. Sidor studies **synapsids** (sih-NAP-sids), and recently went to Antarctica to do some research. We caught up with Dr. Sidor to ask him a few questions about his work.

Q How did you first get interested in paleontology?

A When I was little, my grandmother would bring me to the Peabody Museum at Yale University in Connecticut. I suppose that was my first experience with dinosaurs and other fossils.

Q What are synapsids?

A Synapsids are a group of animals that include mammals and all of their extinct relatives, all the way back to where the mammal and reptile groups split. Since people are mammals, that means you and I are synapsids, too.

Q What's the most interesting thing about studying synapsids?

A One of the interesting things about synapsids is that the earliest ones, like the sailback *Dimetrodon*, lived before dinosaurs. So synapsids have been around for a long time.

Q What's a cool prehistoric animal that you've studied?

A *Lystrosaurus* is a pretty interesting fossil animal. It's been found in Russia, lots of places in Africa, India, Antarctica, and probably in Australia. Since fossils of *Lystrosaurus* have been found on so many continents, it was one of the first land animals to show that all seven of today's continents were part of a giant supercontinent called Pangaea.

Q What was your team looking for on your trip to Antarctica?

A We were trying to understand why land animals haven't been found in Upper Permian [255 million years ago] rocks on Antarctica. It's unusual because, back then, we know that only 1500 miles (2414 km) away there were lots of critters in what is now South Africa.

Q Did you learn anything new from your time there?

A After our fieldwork in Antarctica, we're pretty sure that it was too cold and wet during the Permian to find land animals where we were searching. We found plenty of plant fossils and lots of insect traces, but no bone. But in younger Triassic rock, we found fossil soils with burrows and dens that animals made for the winter.

Dr. Sidor in Antarctica

GLYPTODONTS

Glyptodonts (GLIP-toe-dahnts) were some of the strangest mammals ever and lived 2 million years ago in the Pleistocene. Just like their modern-day armadillo cousins, glyptodonts had dome-shaped bodies covered in armor with a bony patch on their heads like a helmet. Some glyptodonts were as small as 20 inches (51 cm) long, but some were more than 10 feet (3 m) long—like a car-sized armadillo!

Glyptodonts were herbivores, and munched on grass and plants using special grinding teeth in the back of their powerful jaws. With short, thick legs and big feet, glyptodonts weren't light on their toes. Scientists think that these ancient animals moved very, very slowly—a whopping 2 miles (3 km) per hour. And even though a glyptodont was slow, it wasn't an easy meal. Along with all that armor, it had a thick, bony tail to whack any meat-eater who tried to make it a quick snack.

A glyptodont definitely wasn't fast food!

Panochthus (pan-NOCK-thuss), **a glyptodont.**

MORE DINO ADVENTURES COMING SOON!

Well, we've come to the end of our travels—and it's been a wild ride! We got a sneak peek at what life on Earth has been like for the past 542 million years and met tons of amazing ancient animals. But there's still so much more to see! Join us again soon for more dino-mite adventures!

Ground sloth skeleton